JOHN COUTTS

LIVING THE FAITH

Jewish Lives

OLIVER & BOYD

Acknowledgements
The author would like to thank all those who have helped him to write this book, and especially Lady Amelie Jakobovits for telling the story recorded in 'From fear to freedom'.

Thanks are also due to Stuart Polak of the Jewish Board of Education, to Rabbi A. Forta and Rabbi S. Lew, and to Ester Russell who helped explain what it means to 'live the Jewish faith'.

The publishers thank the following for permission to reproduce photographs on the pages listed:
Keter Publishing House, Jerusalem : from *Encyclopaedia Judaica* (pp. 11,14,19,40); *Diaries of Sir Moses and Lady Montefiore*, vol. I, 1890 (p.13); BIPAC (pp. 21,44); Lady Jakobovits (pp. 24,34); Topham (p.25); Juliette Soester (pp. 29,42,46); Yad Vashem, Jerusalem (p. 30); Lubavitch Foundation (p.38); Werner Braun (p.50).

Illustrations by Richard Scollins

A description of the life of Sir Moses Montefiore which includes extracts from his diaries is published in *Sir Moses Montefiore 1785-1885* by Myrtle Franklin and Michael For, Anthony Blond, 1984.

Oliver & Boyd
Robert Stevenson House
1-3 Baxter's Place
Leith Walk
Edinburgh EH1 3BB
A division of Longman Group UK Ltd

ISBN 0 05 004319 6

Typeset on Apple Macintosh Plus in Palatino 11/15 pt.
Produced by Longman Group (F. E.) Ltd.
Printed in Hong Kong

Contents

TIME CHART

ABRAHAM : 1750 BCE (?)

MOSES : captivity in Egypt, Exodus 1250 BCE (?)

KING DAVID : about 1000 BCE

Capitivity in Babylon 586-539 BCE

Violation of the Temple by King Antiochus 168-164 BCE

Wars with the Romans 66-70 CE 132-135 CE

The blood libel at Norwich 1144 CE

Lubavitch movement in eastern Europe about 1780 CE

Sir Moses Montefiore knighted 1837 CE

The blood libel at Damascus 1840 CE

Nazi persecution of the Jews 1933-45 CE

Establishment of the State of Israel 1948 CE

INTRODUCTION

This book is an introduction to Judaism. It tells stories of people who have lived and died in the Jewish faith, and of others who live by the Jewish faith today.

The first section recounts the long and distinguished life of Sir Moses Montefiore, who with his wife, Judith, helped to bring about Jewish emancipation in the nineteenth century. Here faith wins through to freedom.

In the second section Lady Amelie Jakobovits describes the escape of her family from the Nazis during the Second World War. Here we encounter the living faith of a twelve-year-old girl in a world of fear.

The third section introduces us to the Lubavitch community in north London. Jewish young people explain what it means to practise their religion in today's world of opportunity and challenge.

The faith and festivals of Judaism are referred to in the stories as follows:

Section 1 The Shema, Torah, The Passover, Psalms, The place of Jerusalem, Wedding Ceremony.

Section 2 The Sabbath, The Story of Sarah, Rachel,The Exodus from Egypt.

Section 3 The Day of Atonement, Hanukah, Purim, Bar/Bat Mitzvah, Mezuzah.

Pupil activities are suggested at the end of each chapter. A word list, giving explanations of Jewish terms or special words which need comment, is provided at the end of the book. Words included in the list are printed in **bold type** in the text.

HISTORICAL BACKGROUND

*T**his*** is a book about Judaism - the religion of the Jews. There are thought to be about fifteen million Jewish people in the world today.

The Jews are a people with a long history, a special culture, and an ancient religion. For many centuries they have been scattered throughout the world. Yet the Jews have managed to preserve their identity as a distinct people wherever they have lived. Their faith in one living God has helped them to do this.

Since 1948 the Jews have had their own State – Israel*, but not all Jews live in Israel, and not all the people of Israel are Jewish. Not all Jews are religious – some may not believe in God at all. But most Jewish people are still proud of their 'Jewishness' and keep some of the customs described in this book. Many Jews love God with all their hearts.

Now let's go back to the beginning!

FATHER ABRAHAM

The Bible records that Abraham lived in Ur in ancient Babylonia. God gave him a command and a promise. 'Leave your native land and your father's house, and go to a country that I am going to show you. I will give you many descendants and make you a great nation. I will bless you and make your name famous, so that you will be a blessing.' (Genesis 12:1-2)

God's command-and-promise to Abraham is called a **covenant**. Jews believe that it is possible to know and serve the one God as Abraham did. The present-day sign of the covenant is the **circumcision** of boy babies.

*Citizens of the present-day State of Israel are called Israelis. The Bible uses the names 'Hebrews' or 'Israelites'.

MOSES AND THE LAW

The Hebrew people went to live in Egypt and, later on, were made slaves.The book of Exodus in the Bible tells how God sent Moses to lead the people to freedom. The message from God to the ruler of Egypt, the Pharaoh, was 'Let my people go.'

The Hebrews made a hurried escape or **exodus** from Egypt, led by Moses. As they fled they came to an area which was usually under water. The place was called in Hebrew the '**Sea of Reeds**'. On that day the people were able to cross safely. Their pursuers also tried to cross, and they were drowned. Every year, the Jews keep the Feast of the Passover in memory of their escape from slavery.

Moses led the people to Mount Sinai where, according to the Book of Exodus (20:1-17), God gave him the Ten Commandments which are at the heart of the Jewish Law, the **Torah**. So Jews believe that these laws came to them from God; they are not simply rules made by people. Through these laws, God has become known to Jews and to non-Jews as well.

KING DAVID

When the Israelites entered the land of Canaan (modern Israel/Palestine) they had to fight many enemies. King David captured Jerusalem (also called **Zion)** and made it a holy city. He was the leader who made the Israelites into a strong and mighty nation. David's son Solomon built the first Temple in the city of Jerusalem. Here God was worshipped with the sacrifice of animals and with the singing of psalms. The psalms have been translated into many languages, and are still popular today.

'The Lord is my shepherd
I shall not want ...
Surely goodness and mercy shall follow me
All the days of my life,
And I shall dwell in the house of the Lord for ever.'

(Psalm 23: vv 1,6)

A LONG EXILE

But Jerusalem was destroyed, and the Temple burned.The Jews were taken captive in Babylon. They sang a song about that too.

'By the rivers of Babylon, we sat down,
There we wept when we remembered Zion ...
How can we sing a song to the Lord in a foreign land?'
(Psalm 137: vv 1,3)

When the Jews were able to return home their independence lasted only a short time. They were conquered and ruled by the Romans. They fought for their freedom in a terrible war which lasted from 66-70 CE, but they were defeated. Yet again the Temple was destroyed. In the following century the Roman emperor, Hadrian, built a temple to the Roman god Jupiter on the site where the earlier Temple had been.

The Jews were scattered. They became a nation without a country. They were the Jews of the **diaspora,** or 'dispersion'. But the faith was kept alive. The Jews no longer had a Temple, but they came together in meeting-houses called **synagogues** to pray, to sing psalms and to hear readings from the law of Moses. They kept the rules about food which are found in their holy books (the Bible) and they observed the Sabbath day (Friday evening to Saturday evening) as a day of rest.

For centuries the Jews lived in many countries among people of different religions (mainly **Christianity** and **Islam)**. In these countries the Jews were a religious minority. Often they were accepted and allowed to practise their religion, but sometimes they were disliked and feared because they were different and people found their ways strange. Sometimes the Jews were horribly persecuted. Yet even under torture some of them were heard to say the **Shema**, the fundamental statement of their faith:

'Hear, O Israel, the Lord our God is one Lord,
And you shall love the Lord your God with all your heart ...'
(Deuteronomy 6:4)

What have you remembered?

Unscramble the names and complete the sentences correctly.

1.	GESUGNOYA	obeyed God's call to leave Ur.
2.	RMEJESLAU	means the escape from Egypt.
3.	RABMAHA	built the Temple for the Israelites.
4.	LNSMOOO	is also called ZION.
5.	DXESOU	is a Jewish place of worship.

What do you know?

6. What according to the book of Exodus happened at Mount Sinai?
7. Why was the psalm 'By the rivers of Babylon ...' composed?
8. What did the Roman emperor Hadrian do to the Jews?
9. What is the fundamental statement of the Jewish faith?
10. Explain the difference between an Israelite and an Israeli.

What do you think?

11. 'Jews believe that their Laws are not simply rules made by people.' Do you agree? Are some laws given by God? Which ones?
12. Why have the Jews often been victims of persecution?
13. The Jews became 'a nation without a country'. Is this possible? Must every nation have its own country?

A Hundred Years of Faith and Hope

The Life of Sir Moses Montefiore

In the eighteenth century Jews in Britain were a small community : many had connections with Italy and Portugal. Gradually their situation improved as laws that restricted them were repealed.

No one did more for their cause than Moses Montefiore.

Moses' parents were Italians who lived in London and he was born in Italy in 1784. He went to school in Kennington which at that time was a village on the outskirts of London. Moses left school when he was thirteen years old, and there his formal education ended. At that time Jews, like other minority groups, could not attend universities such as Oxford or Cambridge. They were forbidden to enter Parliament or become lawyers. Many Jews found a career in business, and young Moses was apprenticed to a tea merchant in the City of London. This meant a long day's work and a long walk home at the end of it.

Business was booming in London. The 'City' was an international centre for banking and finance. Jewish businessmen played an important part, although only twelve Jews were licensed to practise as **brokers.** In 1807 young Moses received a special present from his uncle who bought him a permit to be one of the twelve Jewish brokers. Used wisely, this permit could prove a passport to riches.

Moses Montefiore was a loyal Jew. He joined a synagogue in London, and kept the **Sabbath** as a day of rest as Jewish law commanded. But he was also loyal to Britain and thought that British Jews should go 'softly softly' in their efforts to be treated in the same way as other citizens. He believed very strongly that Jewish people should be treated equally – they should have full **civil rights** – but he knew also that this would take a long time to achieve.

Britain was then at war with France,and in 1809 Moses took a step which was unusual for a Jew in those days. He became a part-time soldier – a Captain in the Surrey **militia.** For three years he exercised and drilled with his troop. They were ready for the French to invade the British Isles. But the French never did invade. The Emperor Napoleon marched his armies to the east of Europe and in 1812 he had a very bad year! His troops were defeated in the terrible retreat from Moscow and the danger to Britain was removed. 1812 was a very good year indeed for Moses Montefiore. In that year he married Judith Cohen, and the marriage was to be a long and happy one.

Moses Montefiore as a Captain in the Surrey militia

At a Jewish wedding special blessings are recited:

'O make these loved companions to rejoice, even as of old thou didst gladden thy creatures in the garden of Eden. Blessed art thou, O Lord, who makest bridegroom and bride to rejoice.'

This blessing came true for Moses and Judith. At their wedding a prayer shawl, the **Tallith,** was held over their heads. Moses kept this shawl throughout his life, and it was held over *his* head when he died. He was one hundred years old. Over thirty years after the wedding Moses wrote in his diary, 'The Almighty God of Israel in his goodness blessed me with my dear Judith. And a kinder and better wife never existed.'

Two days after the wedding Judith wrote, 'the sort of religion which he possesses ... in my opinion is most essential – a fellow-feeling and **benevolence.**' Judith's own faith was firm. She could read and translate Hebrew, and she spoke French, German and Italian fluently. Judith supported many of Moses' missions and accompanied him on most of them. They shared the same vision of justice for all people, and they faced the many dangers of overseas travel in the cause of Jewish freedom.

Also in 1812 Moses began to work with Nathan Meyer Rothschild – the leading **financier** of the day. It was Rothschild who provided the money to pay the British Army to fight Napoleon. Rothschild had his own international news service, including carrier pigeons, and when Napoleon escaped from the island of Elba in 1815, Rothschild was first to get the news. He rode immediately to Downing Street to tell the Government. Moses was woken with the grim news at five in the morning.

Napoleon lost his last battle at Waterloo in 1815 – due in part to the financial arrangements of Rothschild. In the postwar years Moses Montefiore was in the thick of the business world. He financed the first attempts to supply cities with gas light. When the Provincial Bank of Ireland was formed, he paid out the first notes over the counter in Dublin. He was a Director of the South Eastern Railway Company, the Imperial Brazilian Mining Company, the British Colonial Silk Company and many others. He certainly believed the words he wrote in his diary: 'No man can be happy who does not devote at least five or six hours daily to some useful employment.'

But Moses and Judith together had interests that went much deeper than business ventures. They were concerned to help the victims of slavery and poverty, and cared very much about Jewish communities throughout the world. Their lives were lived by the commandments of the Jewish faith. They tried to get away from London in order to keep the Sabbath in peace, and year by year, they celebrated the Feast of the **Passover.**

Judith Cohen

At Passover time Jews share a special meal, which recalls how their ancestors escaped from Egypt in the time of Moses and how the angel of death 'passed over' them but killed the first-born of the Egyptians (Exodus 12:13). Each part of the meal has a meaning. For example, bread baked without **leaven** (yeast) reminds them that when they fled from Egypt there was no time to bake properly, and **bitter herbs** recall the pain of slavery. Wherever Jewish people live in the world, they always remember the holy city of the old country, Jerusalem. The toast at the Passover meal was, and is still, 'Next year – in Jerusalem.'

In 1827 the dream came true for Moses and Judith. They went to Jerusalem. Years later at Passover time, Moses used to read out an entry from his diary which told how it happened.

'Last night I dreamed I saw in front of me a venerable man whom I knew to be Elijah the prophet. He pointed to Jerusalem which I recognised in the distance ... I resolved the very first thing I would do when I had time would be ... to go to the Holy Land.'

In those days it took twelve hours to reach Dover from London by horse-drawn coach. Three months later travellers might land in Malta, and six weeks after that they would finally arrive on the shores of Palestine.

Moses and Judith see Palestine for the first time

When the Montefiores finally reached Jerusalem, Judith wrote in her diary: 'Many were the solemn thoughts that arose in our minds – finding ourselves ... in this holy land – the country of our ancestors, of our religion, and of our former greatness ...' That visit to Jerusalem helped to change the direction of their lives. Moses wrote in his diary too:

'October 24 (1827). This day I begin a new era. I fully intend to devote much more time to the welfare of the poor and to attend synagogue as regularly as possible ....'

They had some adventures on the way home. Greeks and Turks were at war and their ship was stopped by Turkish gunboats. They also ran into a heavy storm ...

'Since Friday last we have encountered continual gales of wind, with a heavy storm. A little before noon, I threw into the sea a small piece of my last year's Passover cake – asking the Almighty to protect us ...

It is with the warmest gratitude that I humbly acknowledge the Almighty's intervention on our behalf ... the clouds have, as it were by a miracle, dispersed ...'

In later years, Moses read that extract from his diary on the first night of the Passover Festival. Their own escape from danger made Judith and Moses feel very close to their ancestors. They now knew what it felt like to be 'delivered' from danger and death.

In 1831 the Montefiores bought a fine house at Ramsgate in Kent. There they were able to build their own synagogue to celebrate the Sabbath and Holy Days. In 1836 Moses was elected President of the Board of Deputies of British Jews, which made him the leading member of the Jewish community in Britain. In 1837 he was offered the post of High Sheriff of London and Middlesex. This was a great honour, as it was one of the few public offices open to a Jew at the time. But the date of the ceremony to instal Moses as Sheriff clashed with the Jewish New Year. Moses stuck to his Jewish principles.

He wrote, 'I shall have to walk to Westminster instead of going in my state carriage – nor shall I be able to dine with my friends at the inauguration dinner which is given on the 30th of September. I shall endeavour to persuade my colleagues to change it to the 5th of October.' He would not change his mind. 'Let them call me a bigot if they like' he said. His colleagues changed the date of the dinner!

The High Sheriff had many different duties. Amongst them, he had to plan the Lord Mayor's Day parade and visit Newgate Prison. One task was pleasant - the other one was grim. Moses was against capital punishment, which was quite common in those days. No one was executed in London while he was Sheriff. An even greater honour followed Moses' appointment as High Sheriff. He was made a Knight by the young Queen Victoria ...

'On my kneeling to the Queen, she placed a sword on my right shoulder and said, "Rise, Sir Moses!" I had the pleasure of seeing my banner with 'Jerusalem' floating proudly in the hall.'

It was – he declared – the proudest day in his life, apart from his wedding day and the dedication day of the synagogue at Ramsgate.

And so Sir Moses arose – successful, and respected by Jew and

"Arise, Sir Moses!" The young Queen Victoria makes a new Knight

non-Jew alike. His career seemed to show that if Jewish people worked slowly and quietly, prejudice and discrimination against them would simply disappear.

Then, in 1840, an event took place far away from London and Sir Moses. This event was to show that terrible prejudice against Jewish people still existed, and was as bad as anything that had gone before. Sir Moses became deeply involved.

THE BLOOD LIBEL OF DAMASCUS

One of the strangest murder mysteries in history took place in Damascus in the year 1840.

The ancient city of Damascus – capital of Syria – was deeply divided. At that time the city was under the rule of Mehemet Ali of Egypt. Jewish and Christian minorities lived in a town governed by **Muslims.** For thirty-three years a Roman Catholic priest called Father Thomas had been working in Damascus. On 5 February 1840 he went out into the city with his servant and was never seen again. To this day no one knows what became of them.

Rumour got to work. Soon it was whispered – and then shouted – that the Christian Father Thomas had been murdered by Jews who needed human blood to celebrate the Feast of the Passover. This was the 'blood libel' – and it had a long and terrible history.

In the days when the Temple stood in Jerusalem, non-Jews were puzzled by it. There was no image of a God inside (images were forbidden by the second of the Ten Commandments) so why have a temple at all? It was claimed that the Jews used to kidnap a foreigner, and fatten him up for use as a human sacrifice.

Later on the 'blood libel' accusation was made against the Christians, too. Their Holy Communion service spoke of the 'body' and 'blood' of Jesus. Did this mean they were cannibals? Some Romans thought they were.

When Christianity became the religion of the majority of people in Europe, the 'blood libel' charge was thrown back at the Jews. In 1144 it was claimed that Jews in Norwich had kidnapped a little boy called William and crucified and tortured him to imitate the sufferings of Jesus. Through the centuries, the 'blood libel' against the Jews persisted. The Damascus outbreak in 1840 was one in a long line of such accusations.

A mob assembled in the Jewish quarter, shouting that the Jews had murdered Father Thomas. The cry was taken up by Count Ratti-Menton, the French consul in the city, who persuaded the Governor of Damascus, Sherif Pasha, to act.

Someone said Father Thomas had been seen entering a barber's house. The barber denied it. He was thrown into a dungeon and 'persuaded' to name names. Bones were brought forward as evidence, but doctors declared that they belonged to a sheep! Several leading Jews were arrested. They denied all knowledge of the crime. They too were flogged and tortured, and two of them died. Suspicion fell on six more Jews, one of whom was an Austrian citizen. The Austrian consul refused to hand him over to the city authorities. The French consul, Ratti-Menton, had gone too far to take back his charges. He demanded that the prisoners should be executed. Sherif Pasha applied to Mehemet Ali in Cairo to confirm the death sentences.

SIR MOSES ARRIVES

When the news reached Britain it caused great anxiety. In London Jews and non-Jews held a meeting to protest '... that there have been lately revived in the East, those false and atrocious charges so frequently brought against the Jews during the Middle Ages...'

Sir Moses was asked to lead a group of people who were to travel to see Mehemet Ali, ruler of Egypt, who had the power to set free the prisoners in Damascus. With his wife Judith, Moses set out for Egypt. They travelled across France by coach, and then by sailing ship to Malta and Egypt.

Mehemet Ali received the party politely, but the politics of the situation were complicated. The French felt that they had to support their consul, Ratti-Menton. They also thought Sir Moses' concern for the Jewish prisoners was not quite what it seemed to be. They suspected that he was there because the British wanted an excuse to interfere in the politics of the Middle East. The French representative in Alexandria, Cochelet, proposed a way out. Mehemet Ali should declare that the Jews who had already died were guilty of the murder of Father Thomas, but that those still in prison were all innocent and should be set free.

Sir Moses meets Mehemet Ali

Sir Moses Montefiore was disgusted. He said, 'I would sooner die than consent. One of the unhappy men died with the words of the **Shema** on his lips ...' and he asked permission to go to Damascus himself.

At last a compromise was found. Sir Moses would agree not to go to Damascus – and Mehemet Ali would issue a decree. This was to proclaim that the Jews were innocent of the death of Father Thomas, and that they did not use human blood in their religious ceremonies.

But when the decree was written out, it contained an Arabic word meaning 'Pardon'. This implied that the prisoners had committed the crime, and were guilty. Sir Moses would not accept the decree. At last the words were changed to 'honourable release' and the prisoners were set free. It was a famous victory.

Or was it? All but two of the accused failed to recover from their tortures, and many people still believed that they were guilty. A memorial stone to Father Thomas was erected in a church in Damascus, and it declared that he had been 'murdered by Hebrews'. On several occasions Sir Moses Montefiore tried to have the stone taken down, but it stayed in place until 1860, when the church and the stone were destroyed in a riot.

A LIVING LEGEND

For the rest of his life Sir Moses Montefiore travelled and worked for the cause of Jewish freedom and for human rights in general. He went to Morocco, Italy, Spain and Russia. Judith accompanied Moses on his travels. They worked together until Judith was too ill to travel. She died in 1862, on the eve of the Jewish New Year. Her tomb at Ramsgate was a copy of the tomb of Rachel* in Palestine. Judith and Moses had seen the tomb on their first visit to Palestine. It was neglected and in poor condition, and Judith had paid to have it repaired.

On his last visit to Jerusalem, at the age of ninety-four, Moses looked forward to a return by Jews to their ancient homeland.

'It has been my constant dream,' he said, 'I do not expect that all Israelites will quit their abodes, but Palestine must belong to the Jews and Jerusalem is destined to be the seat of the Jewish empire.'

When he could no longer travel he wrote letters in support of the Jewish dream of a homeland, and as always, he prayed for it. In 1880, at the age of ninety-six, he heard that groups of people had set

*You can read about Rachel in the Bible, Genesis 29.

Rachel's tomb. Judith's tomb at Ramsgate is a copy of this

up anti-Jewish leagues, or societies, in Berlin. Saddened by this anti-Semitic feeling, Moses wrote, 'I hope that by prudence and discretion on our part, and increased enlightenment based on principles of humanity among non-Israelites, an improvement in the condition of our brethren will be effected....We must always bear in mind that "it is not by might nor by power" that Israel prevails, "but by the spirit of the Lord of Hosts".'

As he lay dying Moses Montefiore recited words from the Psalms. When he died they held over his head the Prayer shawl that had been used at his wedding.

What have you remembered?

Join these sentences correctly.

1. Not more than 12 Jews were allowed to work as	carrier pigeons
2. Nathan Meyer Rothschild was first with the news by using	a sheep
3. In a dream Moses Montefiore saw	Rachel
4. Damascus was ruled from Egypt by	brokers in the City of London
5. The bones that were said to belong to Father Thomas really belonged to	the prophet Elijah
6. Judith Montefiore restored the tomb of	Mehemet Ali

What do you know?

Complete the sentences using the correct words.

7. On Moses Montefiore's banner was written
   a) 'Let my people go!'
   b) 'Jerusalem'
   c) 'The Lord our God is one Lord'
   d) 'The Lord is my shepherd'

8. The 'blood libel' is
   a) a message written in blood
   b) the ritual murder of a child
   c) the false story that Jews use human blood to celebrate the Passover
   d) a Nazi newspaper

9. A covenant is
   a) a group of witches
   b) a solemn agreement
   c) a community of nuns
   d) a small Jewish temple

10. At the Passover Festival Jews celebrate
   a) passing over the Sea of Reeds
   b) their deliverance from Egypt in the time of Moses
   c) the building of the Temple
   d) the great deeds of King David

11. The Board of Deputies of British Jews is
   a) a committee to help persecuted Jews
   b) the group that runs a synagogue
   c) a committee of Jewish businessmen
   d) the organisation that represents the Jewish community in Britain

What do you think?

12. Sir Moses Montefiore refused to attend a banquet because it clashed with the Jewish New Year. Was he right? How far should you go in sticking to your principles?
13. Sir Moses thought that a dream was guidance from God. Do you agree? In what other ways do people believe that God guides them?
14. Sir Moses thanked God for answering his prayer and saving himself, his wife, and the ship's crew in a storm. What do you think about prayer? Does God answer? How?
15. Why do people believe wicked stories like the blood libel? What other false rumours are believed nowadays?
16. 'Jerusalem is destined to be the seat of the Jewish empire.' Has the creation of the State of Israel made this dream come true? What about the Palestinians?

More things to do

Find out about the Passover meal and its meaning.
Why do the Jews eat unleavened bread and bitter herbs? What are the other special foods and what do they mean?

FROM FEAR TO FREEDOM

The childhood of Lady Amelie Jakobovits

Lady Amelie Jakobovits in 1987

"I really feel as if I've been born twice over. I've had two lifetimes. That's what it can mean to be Jewish in the twentieth century ..."

These are the words of Lady Amelie Jakobovits who had agreed to tell me the terrible and wonderful story of her escape from the Nazis during the Second World War. It's getting on for forty-five years ago now – but she remembers it as clearly as yesterday. Now she's the wife of the Chief Rabbi of the British Commonwealth – but then she had a false name, hid in the forest like a hunted animal, and tried to comfort a baby brother who wouldn't stop crying, not even when the Nazis were near.

NOWHERE TO HIDE

In 1940 the German armies invaded France. The British Expeditionary Force retreated to the sea and managed to escape from Dunkirk. The French government, defeated, signed an armistice. Northern France was to be occupied by the conquerors, while the south would remain under French rule from the town of Vichy. Many refugees left Paris at the time and headed for the unoccupied south. It was safer not to wait for the Nazis to arrive.

Since 1933 Germany had been ruled by Adolf Hitler and his Nazi party. Hitler was no ordinary dictator. His rule was based on the theory that white people in general and Germans in particular were the 'Master Race' whose destiny was to rule the world. He believed that the 'Master Race' had a right – and a duty – to conquer other races, all of which were considered lesser than these superior people. He also believed that they had a right – and a duty – to do something about the Jews.

According to this Nazi theory, the Jews were to blame for Germany's defeat in the First World War and many of the world's troubles. In his book *Mein Kampf* (My Struggle) he had written 'There is no such thing as coming to an understanding with the Jews. It must be "Either – or.'

When the Nazi armies occupied Paris it was 'either – or' for the French Jews – either get out, or risk being sent to a concentration camp. The risk was especially high if you were a well-known Jew – a leader, a teacher or a **Rabbi.** And so Rabbi Munk and his wife fled from Paris with their four children. They lived a wandering life in the south of France. For a while they took refuge in Toulouse, and then in Nice, which was controlled by the Italian army.

The Italians left the Jews alone. But later on, Hitler's armies occupied the whole of France and began to round up 'undesirable' people, like Jews and gypsies. A 'final solution' was eventually proposed for the 'Jewish problem'. All Jews were to be sent to concentration camps. The world now knows that millions of Jews were exterminated in gas chambers at those camps.

Jews being taken away by the Nazis in Germany, 1933

At this time Amelie Munk was twelve years old. There was little chance for her to go to school, and three times a week she would get up at three o'clock in the morning and set off on her bicycle to visit farms in the country. She would come back with a little food – a couple of eggs, some tomatoes, a few potatoes. Though only twelve years old, Amelie seemed older. She already knew about hunger, danger, police checkpoints. And soon her parents were going to need her even more – because her mother became pregnant again.

People laughed. What a time to have another baby! It was a hard time for Amelie's mother. She must have felt like Sarah in the Bible (Genesis 18:11-12) who laughed bitterly when she was told that she would have a child late in life. There was no money for the doctor, and there were no proper medical facilities. Amelie's mother had a difficult, painful pregnancy, and the 'baby' turned out to be twins! That gave people something more to laugh at – and there were many unfriendly eyes watching – people who didn't like Jews – people who would drop a hint to the Nazi headquarters ...

And so, at twelve years old, Amelie had to run the household, do the washing and mending, and care for the family. Her mother had enough to do, coping with the twins.

Every day began and ended with prayer:

'Blessed be the Lord by day. Blessed be the Lord by night.
Blessed be the Lord when we lie down. Blessed be the Lord when we rise up.
Behold, he who guards Israel will neither slumber nor sleep.'

Was God really guarding them?

Their faith was soon to be tested. One Monday morning Rabbi Munk went to the synagogue. As orthodox Jews, the Munk family still practised their religion. A minimum of ten men is needed to form a congregation, and there were still ten Jewish men in Nice. That day, one of them was to give Rabbi Munk terrible news.

This man had been giving lessons on Judaism without permission. The Nazis had found out and had taken him to their headquarters. He had been released after a warning. But while he was listening to the warning he looked down at the desk in front of him. On it lay a file with the name MUNK written across it.

For a moment the Nazi official was called out of the office. The young man took a chance and had a quick look in the file. It said 'Rabbi Munk and family to be arrested at 9.15 on Wednesday and deported to Germany.'

That night Rabbi Munk did not come home. The family had no idea where he had gone. But on Tuesday morning the doorbell rang and there stood a man in a dirty cap and old jacket. His hands and fingernails were grimy. "Mummy," said Amelie, "Here's a man to see you." The man began to cry. It was Rabbi Munk and his own daughter had failed to recognise him because his beard had been cut off! Amelie had never seen her father cry before.

The Rabbi had been to see the *Maquis* – the French resistance movement. He had new documents for all the family – fake birth certificates and ration cards and passports. They also had a new name. The Munks were now the 'Martins'.

"We leave tonight," he said. "We travel separately to the Swiss border. Then the *Maquis* will take us over the frontier and we'll be safe."

Her father and mother took the twins, while Amelie travelled with the other children. The train was crowded – it kept starting and stopping. Nazi soldiers patrolled, checked the passengers, looked at documents. Surely some of them would see through the young 'Martins'? But if they did, they said nothing.

Speaking nearly fifty years later, Lady Jakobovits believes that God was taking care of the family at that time. Even the baby twins flourished!

At 11 o'clock on that Tuesday night, the 'Martin' family met up at a lonely farmhouse near the Swiss border. All had gone well. Their only fear was that a Nazi dog patrol might come round, but they expected their French guides to lead them safely over the frontier to freedom. The guides never came. The Swiss border – and safety – was so near and yet so far. In the grey light of Wednesday morning the family still waited at the farm. All they could do was make their way back to the town of Aix-les-Bains. That meant hitch-hiking – and that was dangerous. A 'friendly' driver could turn you in to the enemy.

Back in Aix-les-Bains the 'Martins' checked into a hotel. It was Friday, and at dusk the Jewish Sabbath began. And the Sabbath day must always be kept as a day of rest, except when life is in danger.

"I guess the Jewish people have survived," said Lady Jakobovits, "because we're people of great hope." Hope made Rabbi Munk/Martin take his ten-year-old son Jackie by the hand and go for a walk round Aix-les-Bains ... "I'm simply bound to meet another Jew," he said.

Within five minutes a man came up and said, "Can I help you?" The French resistance had done their job well. The man failed to see that the scruffy-looking Martin was really a man he knew well in Paris – in fact his own Rabbi! But the Rabbi certainly recognised *him*! Jew had met Jew. There was still hope.

For Lady Jakobovits this was much more than a coincidence. She sees it as a sign of God's mercy, the mercy which is celebrated on the Sabbath day when Jewish people light the Sabbath lamp and say:

> 'Blessed art thou O Lord our God, King of the universe, Who have made us holy by your commandments and commanded us to kindle the Sabbath light.'

Lighting the Sabbath candles. A mother and daughter together

"Come with me," said the man to his Rabbi. "A small group of us are going to say the Sabbath Prayers together."

After prayers the people asked the Rabbi, "Where are you staying?"

"In the Hotel Plaza."

"You must be crazy. It's the Nazi Headquarters."

"So much the better – that's the one place where they'll never think to look for us."

So the game of life and death began all over again. The small Jewish community in Aix-les-Bains had to look for another group of *Maquis* to help the 'Martin' family across the frontier.

Once again a deal was arranged. The helpers were well paid for their assistance. Once again the time and place were fixed. Once again the family split up. On the Sunday morning, the Munk children took the long walk to the lonely farmhouse. A lorry came along, carrying a huge load of hay. Amelie waved it down for a lift. In those days people had a terrible choice: never trust a soul, for someone may betray you. But if you don't trust somebody, you may never escape!

This little boy did not escape from the Nazis

The young driver smiled at Amelie. He knew who they were. And Amelie knew that he knew. Surely he could be trusted?

The family met again at that lonely farm, so close to the Swiss border. It was a warm September day. The sun went down, the darkness closed in. They waited and prayed and hoped, and at a quarter to eleven, the guides from the *Maquis* arrived. They were two huge men, with a couple of guns each. And they gave strict instructions to the family.

"We must walk through the forest to reach the frontier. The Nazis come round on patrol, with dogs. We'll go in front. If we turn round, then lie down flat. Don't make a noise – don't even whisper. It's half an hour's walk."

The two *passeurs* – smugglers of human beings – took the twins on their shoulders. Amelie walked beside her father. He had a small psalm book in his hand, and his lips moved as he read in Hebrew ...

'When the Lord brought back the captives to Zion
We were like men who dreamed.
Our mouths were filled with laughter,
And our tongues with songs of joy ...'

(Psalm 126)

For centuries the psalms have given people hope and faith, but the reading stopped when the guides turned round. They lay flat, listening for the barking of the Nazi dogs. No one made a sound, not even the five-year-old. Then they went forward again, through the warm September night.

Once again the two guides turned round. Once again the fugitives lay still, face down, in the stillness of the forest. Creatures were being hunted that night. The owl was searching for the field mouse, and the fox for the rabbit. Human beings were being hunted too.

Again the guides went forward. Again they stopped .

"Just wait here," they said – and disappeared.

A moment of panic now – fear through your whole body! You never knew whom you could trust in those days. Would the guides ever come back? If they did come back, would they bring the Nazis?

The guides returned. "It's twelve minutes to midnight," they said. "The Nazi patrols usually come round in a few minutes' time. The fence is 200 metres ahead. We've cut a hole in the wire. All you have to do is creep through the hole and walk down the hill. Then you're in Switzerland. And now ... HANDS UP!"

The guides had been well paid. But now they proceeded to rob the refugees of everything they could take. Ration cards, identity documents – all were handed over. They took a box of matches from the Rabbi, and the wedding ring from Mrs Munk. "Open your mouths," they said to the grownups. They were checking for gold teeth. Then they vanished.

"Now we are really like dogs," said Rabbi Munk to Amelie. "We've nothing left in life that belongs to us except our skin."

The family went slowly forward to the barbed wire. Had it really been cut? The guides had kept that part of their promise at least. There was a gap. In spite of wearing two sets of clothes they were all badly scratched. Sore and aching, they struggled on and rolled down the hill.

But then there was the river! No one had told them about the river. If the river was the frontier, they were still on French territory! It was too dark to tell how deep the water was, and Amelie's mother couldn't swim. If only they had a box of matches – just to see if there was a way through. They were like the Israelites trapped by the Sea of Reeds. There was nothing they could do. So they lay down in the warm night and waited.

And then Marc, one of the twins, began to cry. Marc had always been a contented child. He had even sat quietly on the shoulders of the guides. But now he cried and cried. They cuddled him, they soothed him. They took turns to walk him up and down the river bank. But still he cried. In the still forest the sound would travel a long way. Amelie had got to know her father well in those terrible months. Now, close beside him, she could feel his desperation. Surely the Nazi patrols would hear!

Amelie looked up. "There's a light!" she exclaimed. The Rabbi put his hand over her mouth ...

The light gleamed and disappeared. Then it flashed again – surely it was nearer? A third time – closer still! As they lay pressed close to the ground, they could feel something – or someone – approaching them. A body fell over them. Then the light was turned round to show a uniform. A man's voice spoke.

"I'm a Swiss soldier," he said. "Follow me."

The soldier led them to the river. It was only waist deep. Taking the twins on his shoulders he carried them through. Then he went back for their mother. He led the family up a hill to a road – and they were safe at last.

"I am the father of ten children," said the soldier. "I just couldn't bear to hear the baby crying. So I asked my commanding officer's permission to come and look for you ... Welcome to Switzerland."

Amelie Munk (left) and her brothers and sisters after their escape!

AND AFTERWARDS ...

The Munk/Martin family stayed in Switzerland till the end of the war. Then they returned to Paris, where Rabbi Munk began work again with what was by then a very small Jewish community. Amelie worked hard to catch up on her studies!

One day a yound Rabbi – Immanuel Jakobovits – came over from Ireland for a holiday. Amelie showed him the sights of Paris ...

After their marriage they lived in Ireland and had five children. Then followed a move to London where Amelie's husband – now Lord Jakobovits – became the Chief Rabbi of the British Commonwealth.

"If the baby hadn't cried the soldier would never have come," Lady Jakobovits recalled. "Then the Nazi patrols with their dogs would have caught us on the wrong side of the river. It was just like the story of our mother Sarah in the Bible. Everyone laughed at the idea of her having a son at her age. And yet she became the mother of a great nation.

"And I'm now the grandmother of many grandchildren. And the little boy who cried on the river bank has a family of his own."

"All this" – declares Lady Jakobovits – the Amelie Munk who used to be – "is a sure sign of the goodness of God."

What have you remembered?

Complete the sentences correctly.

1. The Nazis rounded up Jews and
   a) policemen
   b) gypsies
   c) Italians
   d) collaborators

2. The minimum number of men needed to form a synagogue is
   a) ten
   b) twelve
   c) fifteen
   d) twenty-five

3. Rabbi Munk began to cry because
   a) his family were in danger
   b) he could not conduct services
   c) he could be arrested at any time
   d) his own daughter did not recognise him

4. The guides stole Amelie's mother's
   a) watch
   b) money
   c) Bible
   d) wedding ring

5. The Swiss soldier found the family because

   a) he was on patrol
   b) he heard the baby crying
   c) he saw a light
   d) Nazi guard dogs were barking

What do you know?

6. What did Adolf Hitler think about the Jews?
7. What was on the secret file in the Nazi headquarters?
8. Why was the Hotel Plaza a good place to stay?
9. What did Amelie's father read as they walked to the frontier?
10. What did Rabbi Munk do after the war?

What do you think?

11. Why did some people believe Hitler's theory about the 'Master Race'?
12. "The Jewish people have survived because we're people of great hope." Do you agree with Lady Jakobovits?
13. Amelie believed that God had helped the family to escape. She knows of course that many others did not escape. What do you think about 'providence' - the idea of God's loving care for each person?
14. Why did the *Maquis* help the family and then rob them?
15. Think of some reasons why many people would have been unwilling to help the Munks.

More things to do

16. Look up the Psalms in the Bible. Find one that fits the situation of the Munk family and copy out two or three key verses.
    (Possible psalms are 23, 43, 90, 130.)
17. Write a radio script for part of this story.
    For example: Amelie on her bicycle – trying to get food; the Sabbath meeting at Aix-les-Bains; the baby crying by the river; the coming of the Swiss soldier.
    People in your class could each read a part and you could record the play on tape.
18. Write a stage play of the scene where the Munks are robbed of everything by the guides.

The Story of Lubavitch

A visit to the London Community Centre

"*This*," said the Rabbi, "is where we hold school assemblies." I could easily imagine that. There was a curtained stage at one end of the large and attractive hall.

I thought of the Head Teacher giving talks to the crowd below, and of concerts and play productions. On the floor were criss-cross red and white lines – markings for volley-ball, and badminton ...

"Take a look behind you," said the Rabbi.

Behind me was something different – it looked like a large wooden cupboard with decorated carvings. A blue curtain hung over the front and there was an inscription in unfamiliar writing on the top.

"Ah yes," I said. "That must be the **Ark.** You keep it at the back."

"No," said the Rabbi. "This is the front. When we use the assembly hall as a synagogue we all turn and face this way. We've also got special acoustic tiles in the ceiling so that you can hear clearly from all parts of the building. That way, we don't need microphones. It makes it much easier on the Sabbath."

I remembered that the Sabbath day (Friday evening to Saturday evening) is special in the Jewish religion. 'Remember the Sabbath Day to keep it holy. You shall labour for six days and do all your work, but the seventh day is a day in honour of the Lord your God.' (Exodus 20: 9-10)

The Sabbath is to be kept as a day of rest – and switching mikes on and off is regarded as work.

Senior school speech day in the Lubavitch school hall

Using the computer at Lubavitch school

I tried to show off by reading the Hebrew writing on top of the Ark. Hebrew runs from right to left. One of the words was

משה

which I knew meant 'Moses.' Rabbi Forta helped me with a complete translation. It reads:

'Moses commanded us the **Torah** as an inheritance for the congregation of Jacob.'

"Come along," said my guide. "Let's go and have a look at the swimming pool ..."

Rabbi Arye Forta had kindly agreed to show me the Lubavitch Community Centre in Stamford Hill, north London. But who – or what – was Lubavitch? And why had it come to Stamford Hill? When I asked Rabbi Forta to explain, he began by taking me back in time, to a place far away from north London ...

A SMALL TOWN IN RUSSIA

I found out that Eastern Europe was a stronghold of Jewish life before the Nazi invasions of the Second World War. Jews formed a large minority in the borderlands between Poland and Russia. Two of the many centres of the Jewish religion were Chernobyl (scene of the nuclear power station accident in 1986) and Lubavitch.

However, the religious life of the ordinary people and that of the scholars was a world apart. Scholars concentrated on the study of the Law, while ordinary folk loved their religion but hardly understood it.

HEAD AND HEART TOGETHER

There is a story that is often told in the Lubavitch community. It is about a Jewish villager who drank too much before the **Day of Atonement.** When he woke up – with a hangover – the opening service had already started. He was too embarrassed to go to the synagogue, and he didn't know the prayers by heart. So he repeated the letters of the Hebrew alphabet over and over again – aleph, beth, gimel, daleth – all through the day, asking God to rearrange the letters into the words of the proper prayers!

On the following day the villager went to the synagogue. Sure enough, the Rabbi asked him why he had been missing the evening before – after all, the Day of Atonement is the most solemn and holy of all Jewish festivals. The man owned up and asked whether his way of saying the prayers could be pardoned.

"Your prayer pleased God more than mine," said the Rabbi, "because you said it with all your heart."

Among the Jewish scholars there were people who wanted to bridge the gap – to join head and heart. One of them, Rabbi Shneur Zalman (1745 - 1813), made this humble comment about himself – 'I know a little about learning and nothing about prayer.' He gathered together a group of disciples who were to be 'lamplighters'. Lamplighters went out to share their learning with others. They would combine prayer with learning and serve God with head and heart. In the nineteenth century the community Rabbi Shneur Zalman founded, which was later centred in the little town of Lubavitch, brought new life to Judaism throughout Eastern Europe. Lubavitch gave its name to a movement which brought together the 'head' and the 'heart' of the Jewish faith.

Rabbi Shneur Zalman

SCATTERED TO THE WINDS!

A terrible fate was to befall the Jews of Eastern Europe. Too often, those who lived in the Russian Empire were the victims of racist attacks called **pogroms** (these happened between 1880 and 1917). But far worse was to follow. In 1939 Nazi Germany overran Poland and attacked the Soviet Union. Hitler then attempted the 'Final Solution' – the total extermination of the Jews. Six thousand Jewish communities were wiped out, and few Jews remain in Lubavitch today. In 1940 Rabbi Joseph Schneerson, then the leader of the Lubavitch movement, arrived in the United States of America. There he began all over again what Rabbi Shneur Zalman did in Eastern Europe. He started to provide Jewish education and arouse interest in Jewish values. Educational centres were set up throughout the USA. The work spread to Europe, South America, Australia, and throughout the world.

Lubavitch came to Britain in 1948. That was a crucial year for Judaism – the destruction of the holocaust had been great and terrible. Many people must have despaired for the future of Jewish life. Could the scattered seeds grow and flourish again?

Back in the Lubavitch centre in London, Rabbi Forta reminded me, "Head comes first and heart must follow. It's no use teaming up with Lubavitch if you aren't willing to work. When I first came here 25 years ago there were two old houses on the site. It was the week before Passover – and we were taking part in a campaign to ensure that Jews throughout the neighbourhood were ready to celebrate the festival. When we got back at 10 o'clock in the evening a team of Rabbis was hard at work – laying floorboards! I was impressed. I was used to thinking that the Rabbis never got their hands dirty."

LUBAVITCH HOUSE SCHOOL

Growth there has certainly been. After leaving Rabbi Forta, I found myself talking to the Head himself, Rabbi S. Lew, while school examinations were going on all around us ...

At the entrance to Rabbi Lew's room I noticed a **mezuzah** – a small box containing a scroll with words from the Bible to remind people of their duty to God. A mezuzah is placed over every room in the school building.

The Lubavitch school now takes in 700 pupils from kindergarten to sixth form. It aims to provide a living Jewish education for the world of today. Half the time is taken up with Jewish studies – but Rabbi Lew explained that his included languages, geography, and even mathematics.

I could tell, from the look of the children and the classrooms, that the school is a happy place. But what is it like to grow up in such a religious atmosphere? How do they celebrate the Jewish festivals? I asked the Head about one of these festivals, **Hanukah** (sometimes spelt Chanukah).

THE MEZUZAH

This is a small container placed on the doorposts of a Jewish home. Inside are written the words of Deuteronomy 6:4-9 and 11:13-21.

Here is an extract:

'Hear O Israel; the Lord our God, the Lord is one. And you shall love the Lord Thy God with all your heart, and with all your soul, and with all your might. And these words, which I command you this day, shall be upon your heart ...
And you shall write them upon the doorposts of your house, and upon your gates.'

A silver Mezuzah symbol on a door post. It is touched by people as they enter the room so it is set at an angle to match the angle of the right hand

HANUKAH

Adolf Hitler was not the first ruler to try to wipe out the Jewish people and their religion. In 167 BCE King Antiochus Epiphanes banned the Jewish faith, vandalised the Temple in Jerusalem and tried to turn it into a centre of idol-worship. Three years later, in 164, it was recaptured by freedom-fighters – the Maccabees. They purified and rededicated the Temple. 'A sacrifice was offered on the new altar in accordance with the law of Moses ... For eight days they celebrated the rededication of the altar.'(1 Maccabees 4: 53,56)

THE ORIGIN OF HANUKAH

The temple is profaned

'On the fifteenth day of the month of Kislev in the year 145 (that is, 167 BCE) King Antiochus set up 'The Awful Horror' on the altar of the temple, and pagan altars were built in the towns throughout Judaea ... Anyone who was caught with a copy of the sacred books, or who obeyed the Law, was put to death by order of the King.'

(from 1 Maccabees 1: 54-57)

The temple is rededicated

'The twenty fifth day of the ninth month, the month of Kislev, in the year 148 (that is 164 BCE) was the anniversary of the day the Gentiles had desecrated the altar. On that day a sacrifice was offered on the new altar in accordance with the Law of Moses ...'

'For eight days they celebrated the rededication of the altar...'

'Then Judas, his brothers, and the entire community of Israel decreed that the rededication of the altar should be celebrated with a festival of joy and gladness at the same time each year ... lasting for eight days.'

(from 1 Maccabees 4: 52-59)
Good News Bible: The Apocrypha

Lighting the Menorah at Hanukah

At Hanukah time the pupils of Lubavitch recall that great day by lighting – a day at a time – the candles on the **Menorah** candlestick. They also enjoy doughnuts and pancakes fried in oil. Even the oil has a special meaning. When the Maccabees won back the Temple – so the story goes – there was only one day's supply of oil left. But by a miracle, it lasted for the whole of the eight-day celebrations. There's all sorts of fun at Hanukah – parties, games and quizzes, as well as the special food.

I liked the sound of Hanukah – so I decided to ask about another festival – **Purim.**

PURIM

The Hanukah candle is lit in school, but Rabbi Lew went on to explain to me that everyone goes to the synagogue for Purim. Purim recalls the time when the Jews were saved from persecution, as told in the book of Esther in the Bible.

During the reign of Ahasuerus, King of Persia (486-465 BCE), the Jewish people were hated by Haman, one of the king's men. Haman quarrelled with a Jew named Mordecai, who had once saved the king's life, because Mordecai would not bow down to him. So in revenge, Haman wanted to get rid of Mordecai and all the Jews. He persuaded the king that the Jews did not obey the laws, and were a danger to the country. The king believed Haman, and he ordered that all the Jews should be killed.

Mordecai told his cousin Esther about this plot, and what was to happen to the Jews, and he asked for Esther's help. Esther was the king's new queen. The king did not know that she was related to Mordecai or that she was Jewish. Esther risked her own life to tell the king about Haman's plotting. If the king had not believed her, he would have had her put to death. But the king did believe Esther! Haman was executed on the gallows which he had had made for Mordecai, and the Jews were saved.

"The danger to the Jews at that time was physical," explained Rabbi Lew, "and so we celebrate in a physical way. We go to the synagogue to hear the story of Esther and whenever the name 'Haman' is mentioned each person can rattle their rattle or blow their whistle or shout 'Boo' very loudly."

I did know that Esther is the only book in the Bible which never once mentions the name of God! But Rabbi Lew told me that God is in the story all the time.

"The name 'Esther' means 'concealment', and God is concealed in the story in the form of Nature." So all the coincidences that led to the defeat of Haman aren't really coincidences at all – they are God's hidden plan in operation.

Celebrating Purim in a synagogue

"That's why we have masquerading at Purim time," explained Rabbi Lew. "Come along to Stamford Hill and you'll see people in disguise – as letter-boxes, animals, parcels – it's all part of the 'concealment' idea."

But Purim time means speaking out as well as hiding. Esther and Mordecai were brave, and spoke out. Every year, at Purim time, the head of the international Lubavitch community broadcasts to the world. For the Lubavitch community has a duty to educate all Jews, and therefore, by extension, all people.

BRICKS OR DIAMONDS?

I could see that you can have fun in Judaism but I wondered whether some people wouldn't find the many rules restrictive.

"You can do anything as long as you do nothing," replied Rabbi Lew. "If you play cricket you can't go swimming. If you write a letter you can't play cricket. You have to choose the things that help – the rules can be a burden but the burden is worth carrying." Then the Rabbi told me an old parable.

Two men are carrying sacks up hill. One man has a sack full of bricks. All he wants to do is to drop a few of them. The other man has a sack – just as heavy – that is full of diamonds. All that man wants is to add a few more diamonds!

MY BEST FRIEND - THE SABBATH DAY

There is no doubt that Rabbi Lew thinks he is carrying a sack of diamonds. And he feels that many of his pupils feel the same way. "Our fourteen-year-olds like their tape-recorders and their personal stereos just like anyone else," he told me, "but when you observe the Sabbath you develop another side of life. You find out what kind of person you can be when deprived of switches and buttons."

Rabbi Lew practises what he preaches. He once got stuck at London's Heathrow Airport on the Sabbath – and stayed there for 24 hours! "I had some food," he told me. "I did some praying. I did some thinking. I learned a lot about the Sabbath. I was a person stranded with my best friend." Then he added, "Mind you, to save life you must break the Sabbath. One of my children was born on the Sabbath, and of course we called the ambulance."

ESTER TODAY

The tape in my machine ran out. Rabbi Lew gave me another one. Then he passed me on to Ester Russell, a former pupil of the school. Ester told me she had been at Lubavitch from kindergarten to the sixth form. Then she went on to Israel to study to be a teacher.

Plainly she had loved her time at the Lubavitch school. "Religion and life go all together," she told me. "It was great."

Then I asked Ester a serious question: "How do you think of God?"

"God is my life," she answered. "I don't just have ten minutes a day when I think of God."

"But you know God through the Bible – the Law of Moses?"

"Not just there. God isn't confined to books. God comes into the thoughts of everyday life. Nothing happens by coincidence. All that God does is for the best – even if it appears bad at the time."

Ester Russell made me think back to Esther in the Bible. She told me again about the idea of God being 'hidden' or 'concealed'. When you wonder what God is doing – when things are bad – that's 'concealed goodness', but in the end things will go well and that will be 'revealed goodness'.

"Not everyone can believe that," I suggested.

"True," she replied, "and not all Jews believe it. But every Jew – even those who don't pray or go to synagogue – keeps a portion of their 'Jewish soul', like the oil that never ran out at the first Hanukah."

SEVEN RULES FOR HUMANITY

I could understand that the Lubavitch community feels it has a mission to help Jews to serve God and humanity. What about the rest of us, I wondered? Ester told me about the Seven Laws of the Sons of Noah, which apply to all people, regardless of race or creed.

1. Worship only one God.
2. Do not take God's name in vain (i.e. do not curse).
3. Do not murder.
4. Do not steal.
5. Do not commit sexual misdemeanours, such as incest and adultery.
6. Do not tear the limb from a living animal. (Ester told me this forbade cruelty to animals.)
7. Set up law courts to see that these rules are kept.

BAR/BAT MITZVAH

But if seven laws apply to everybody, the law of Moses remains a special duty for Jews. Ester told me about **Bar Mitzvah** - when a Jewish boy becomes a 'Son of the Commandment'. At the age of thirteen he is considered old enough to play the part of the grown-up person. So he undertakes a course of preparation and study.

Then the great day comes - the Sabbath after his birthday. During the reading of the Torah, he is called up to recite the Blessings and he reads aloud - in Hebrew - part of the Bible prescribed for the day. It's a solemn and happy day for the boy, his family and his friends. Presents are given and there may be a reception or a party as well.

What about the girls, I wondered, and learned that they become **Bat Mitzvah** - 'daughters of the Commandment'. Customs vary in different communities, but in Lubavitch at least, girls don't read from the scroll of the Law.

"I had a big party", Ester told me, "when I was twelve years old. I was given my own copy of the Scriptures, and I was allowed to go to America to see the Lubavitcher Rebbe. That's the name given to the leader of the world-wide Lubavitch community. At present he is Rabbi Menachem Mendel Schneerson."

But why on her twelfth birthday? I learned that the age is twelve

Monday or Thursday morning service: Bar Mitzvah boy can now read publicly from the Torah

for girls and thirteen for boys because girls are believed to grow up earlier than boys. "My sister has just had her twelfth birthday," Ester told me. "She's celebrated her Bat Mitzvah too. She wrote to the Rabbi to tell him."

"Is it a happy time or a solemn time?" I asked.

"Both. When the celebrations die down you realise what it means."

"Don't you feel cut off from the outside world?" – I wondered. But Ester didn't feel cut off at all. Some of it – the bad side – she was glad to be cut off from! "You see the world in a different light," she told me. "My prayer takes about fifteen minutes and then it keeps me going for the rest of the day."

PRAYER

Ester showed me her book of daily prayer. The prayers are said in Hebrew. "Sometimes, if I was away at camp, say, people might pray together: but most of the time I say the prayers under my breath ... and I pray for others ... that life may be 'revealed goodness' for them and not 'concealed goodness'."

HAPPY DAYS AT SCHOOL

I asked Ester to think of a really happy time at Lubavitch House School. She mentioned the school play, when pupils prepared costumes, tickets, production, and – with teachers' help – the script.

"What part did you have?" I asked. I got a surprise.

"King Richard the Lion Heart."

The play was about King Richard, who went on a crusade, captured a Jewish boy, and forced him to serve in the army. This seemed very hard, for the boy was forced to fight against fellow-Jews, but there was 'concealed goodness' in what happened. God always has a secret plan. In the end Richard captured more Jews – and the boy was able to save them. So 'concealed goodness' became 'revealed goodness' after all!

A PRAYER TO KEEP YOU GOING

When I got home I took out my own Jewish prayer book and looked up some of the prayers that Ester uses every day. There was the first of the famous 'Eighteen Benedictions'.

> 'We praise you, O Lord our God and God of our fathers, God of Abraham, God of Isaac and God of Jacob ... You rule your creatures with sovereign mercy and the universe with sovereign might;
> 'You remember the loyalty of our forefathers and, in love, bring redemption to their children's children, for the sake of Your name ...'

I added my own wish, and my own prayer – 'revealed goodness' for Ester, the school she loves, and the whole Lubavitch community.

What have you remembered?

Complete the sentences. Match the words on the left with the words on the right.

1. A **POGROM** is	a prayer-shawl
2. **HANUKAH** is	a festival in commemoration of Queen Esther
3. A **MENORAH** is	an anti-Jewish riot
4. **PURIM** is	a branched candlestick
5. A **TALLITH** is	a festival of lights

What do you know?

6. What was the 'final solution'?
7. When can you take a rattle or a whistle to the synagogue?
8. When is it right to break the Sabbath?
9. What are the Seven Laws of the Sons of Noah?
10. Explain the meaning of the words **BAR/BAT MITZVAH**.

What do you think?

11. "Rules can be a burden but the burden is worth carrying." Do you agree with Rabbi Lew?
12. "When people seem to suffer for no reason then it is 'concealed goodness'." Do you agree with Ester?
13. Ester said, "God comes into the thoughts of everyday life." What do you think?
14. At the age of twelve Jewish girls become 'Daughters of the Law'. Jewish boys become 'Sons of the Law' at thirteen. Is this the right age for young people to be considered responsible?
15. Ester was not sorry to be cut off from some of the bad side of life. What is it best *not* to know about?

More things to do

16. Make a model of a **Mezuzah**. Look up Deuteronomy 6:4 and 11:13. Write the verses out, make a small container, and put them inside.
17. Write your own radio drama based on the story of Esther.

Word List

anti-Semitism	anti-Jewish feelings or behaviour
Ark	a cupboard in a synagogue which holds the scroll of the Law
BCE/CE	'Before the Christian Era', and 'in the Christian Era' (the same as BC/AD)
Bar/Bat Mitzvah	'Son/Daughter of the Law': also the name of the ceremony to mark the time when young Jews accept the duties of a grown-up person. The girls are twelve and the boys thirteen years old
benevolence	blessing, goodness
Bible	the Jewish Bible contains thirty-nine books, written in Hebrew. Non-Jews call it the Old Testament
bitter herbs	most often horseradish. Eaten at Passover time to remind Jews of their time of slavery in Egypt
broker	the person in the middle of a business deal. Brokers put sellers in touch with buyers, and buy and sell for other people. A broker is paid for doing this by the people involved in the deal
Christianity	religion of people who believe that Jesus Christ is the Son of God
circumcision	an operation to remove the foreskin of the penis
civil rights	the belief that all people, whatever their sex, race or religious beliefs, should be treated equally by the laws of a country
Day of Atonement	'Yom Kippur' in Hebrew. The holy day at the beginning of the Jewish year (in autumn) when Jews confess their sins
diaspora	dispersion or 'scattering': it refers to Jewish people who had to leave their country and settle in other lands
Exodus	the departure of the Jews from Egypt. It is also the name of the book in the Bible which describes these events. The word means 'leaving' or 'going out'

financier someone who deals with money matters

Gentiles non-Jews

Hanukah also spelt 'Chanukah': the festival of lights, held in December to celebrate the rededication of the Temple in Jerusalem in 164 BCE

holocaust 1) a sacrifice in which the whole animal was burnt on the altar of the Temple
2) the attempted extermination of the Jews during the Second World War

Islam religion of people who follow the teachings of the prophet Muhammad

inauguration a ceremony marking the beginning of something. Here it marked the start of Moses Montefiore's time as High Sheriff of London

leaven yeast which makes dough rise

matzos special bread which is eaten at Passover. The Jews left Egypt in such a hurry that they had no time to wait for the yeast to work in their bread. So unleavened bread is eaten to remind Jewish people of the time when they escaped from Egypt to freedom

Menorah branched candlestick lit at Hanukah. It has one candle for each day and a 'servant' candle to light the others

Mezuzah a small scroll with words from the Bible. It is placed in a box and attached to the doorpost of a Jewish home

militia people who were not regular soldiers, but who could be called up for military service in times of war. They were a reserve force, and were under the command of the Lord Lieutenant of each county

Muslims followers of the prophet Muhammad. Their religion is called Islam

Passover the spring festival in which Jews remember how their people were freed from slavery in Egypt and how the angel of death 'passed over' them but killed the first-born of the Egyptians

Pogrom an anti-Jewish riot

Purim	the festival when Jews remember how their people were saved from death, as told in the book of Esther. 'Purim' means 'lots'. The festival is called this because lots were cast to decide the day for destroying the Jews (Esther 9: 20-24)
Rabbi	the leader of a Jewish community
Sabbath	the seventh day of the week. A holy day of rest
Sea of Reeds	here the Israelites crossed in safety while the pursuing Egyptions were drowned. Traditionally called the Red Sea (Exodus 13:18)
Shema	'Hear ...': the beginning of the Jewish belief, 'Hear, O Israel, the Lord our God is one Lord ...'
synagogue	a meeting-house or place of worship for Jews
Tallith	a prayer shawl with fringes
Torah	teachings: 1) the Law of Moses, the first five books of the Bible 2) the teaching of the Jewish faith in general
Zion	The name of the hill on which Jerusalem was built.The city itself was sometimes called Zion
Zionism	The movement to set up a Jewish state in the land of Palestine.